S0-ARK-097

SPOTLIGHT INTERACTIVE

STARGAZER

TRACK THE NIGHT SKY FROM YOUR OWN BACKYARD

BY ROBIN SCAGELL

CONTENTS

Thunder Bay Press

An imprint of the Advantage Publishers Group

10350 Barnes Canyon Road, San Diego, CA 92121

www.thunderbaybooks.com

Copyright © The Book Studio, 2008

All notations of errors or omissions should be addressed to Thunder Bay Press, Editorial Dept, at the above address.

All other correspondence (author inquiries, permissions) concerning the content of this book should be addressed to The Book Studio Ltd, Garrard Way, Kettering, Northants NN16 8TD.

ISBN-13: 978-1-59223-956-6

ISBN-10: 1-59223-956-0

Printed in China.

1 2 3 4 5 12 11 10 09 08

Sophisticated satellite ▶
technology constructs a
snapshot view of the
Sun's surface

LOOKING AT THE NIGHT SKY

Most people don't look at the night sky much until something catches their eye—a silvery crescent moon, perhaps, or the majestic constellation of Orion glittering in the January sky. Then a few weeks later you look up and they're no longer there, or maybe a vacation abroad means that you see unfamiliar stars. This book aims to bring the stars to you. Using the novel touch-board and this book, you can identify the stars you see on any night of the year, from any location in the world.

◄ A deepening, clear twilight sky promises a starry night.

The Earth turns within the celestial sphere (left). As seen from a viewpoint on the surface (right), the sky appears to rotate around the celestial pole, which is at an angle to the horizon. In the northern hemisphere, the Pole Star is close to this point. ►

WHY THE STARS CHANGE FROM MONTH TO MONTH

The Earth orbits the Sun, taking a year to do so. As a result, if you look out at the same time each night you'll see a slightly different view. Comparing them, you'll find that the sky moves slightly from east to west night by night. Over the course of a year, you'll see the entire heavens that are visible from your location. But the Earth turns every day as well, also making the Sun, Moon, planets, and stars appear to move from east to west. So earlier in the evening you see stars that a month or two ago were visible at midnight, while if you wait up after midnight you can see the stars that will be coming along in to view in the sky in a month or two.

The sky moves from east to west wherever you are on Earth. But in the southern hemisphere, everything appears upside down compared with the northern hemisphere. The Sun and Moon appear in the north, not the south, and move from right to left instead of from left to right. To see the sky looking toward the pole from wherever you are, use the maps on pages 21 (northern hemisphere) or page 59 (southern).

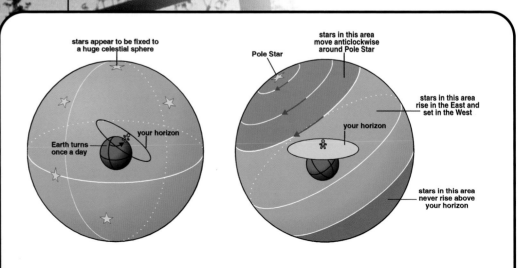

stars appear to be fixed to a huge celestial sphere

Earth turns once a day

your horizon

stars in this area move anticlockwise around Pole Star

Pole Star

stars in this area rise in the East and set in the West

your horizon

stars in this area never rise above your horizon

MOON AND PLANETS

Because the moon and planets change their location all the time, it's not possible to mark them on the star maps. More information about the positions of the planets is given on page 8.

The crescent Moon, Jupiter (right), and ▶ Mars (upper right) seen together in the sky.

The maps apply at the times shown, but also two hours earlier in the evening a month later or two hours later in the evening a month earlier. If you want a sneak preview of what stars will be in the sky in an hour or two, look to the easternmost side of the map.

TIP

The maps apply at the times shown, but also two hours earlier in the evening a month later or two hours later in the evening a month earlier. If you want a sneak preview of what stars will be in the sky in an hour or two, look to the easternmost side of the map.

USING THE TOUCH-BOARDS

Step 1 Face south (in the northern hemisphere), or north (in the southern hemisphere). In the southern hemisphere, use the maps upside down.

Step 2 Choose the map according to your season. Each one applies at about 10 p.m. in the months shown. Each map shows the view from the horizon to overhead.

Step 3 The horizon for your location varies with your latitude, as shown here.

Step 4 The red button in each case highlights the main stars of a Signpost Constellation for the season. Once you've found that, go on to identify the others. Use the pages in the book to find out more about what you can see in each constellation with the naked eye or binoculars.

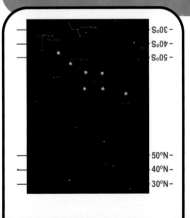

Where your horizon will lie on the touch board. ▶
50ºN is British Columbia, 40ºN is the central
U.S. and 30ºN is the southern U.S.

STARS AND CONSTELLATIONS

Getting to know the stars in the sky can be quite a challenge. When you get away from city lights and gaze up, the sky can be filled with stars. That's just how our distant ancestors from the dawn of history saw it when they sat around their camp fires, telling tales. Back then there were no books and maps of the sky, but they picked out patterns and used them in their stories. We still use many of the same patterns that were named thousands of years ago, and the stories bring a special dimension to our understanding of the sky.

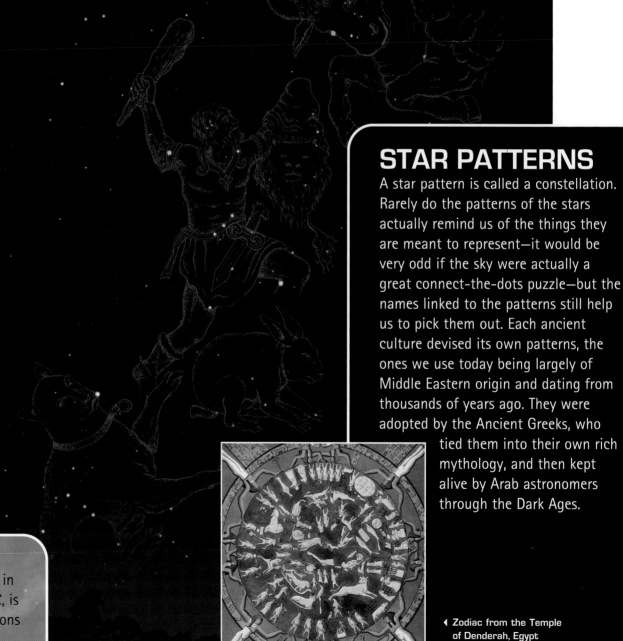

The figures of Canis Major, Orion, ▶ Taurus, and Lepus form an imaginary picture book in the sky around which storytellers could weave legends.

STAR PATTERNS

A star pattern is called a constellation. Rarely do the patterns of the stars actually remind us of the things they are meant to represent—it would be very odd if the sky were actually a great connect-the-dots puzzle—but the names linked to the patterns still help us to pick them out. Each ancient culture devised its own patterns, the ones we use today being largely of Middle Eastern origin and dating from thousands of years ago. They were adopted by the Ancient Greeks, who tied them into their own rich mythology, and then kept alive by Arab astronomers through the Dark Ages.

◀ Zodiac from the Temple of Denderah, Egypt

ASTRO FACT

The ceiling of the Temple of Denderah in Egypt (right), dating from about 50 BC, is one of the earliest known representations of the constellations in their accurate postions.

STAR NAMES

The names of individual stars have come to us from different sources. Some are Greek, many Arabic (those beginning with "Al-," meaning "The"), and some Latin. They often refer to the part of the creature represented by the constellation, but not necessarily the same creature that we refer to today, and have been copied and miscopied by scholars of different nationalities over the ages. Experts still argue over the true origins of some, such as the famous Betelgeuse. As a result, there is often no fixed pronunciation of star names —but they add greatly to the charm of learning the sky.

There are also astronomical designations using the Greek alphabet in which (usually) the brightest star in each constellation is called Alpha, the next brightest Beta, and so on. The constellation name is used in the genitive form, so Betelgeuse in Orion is also known as Alpha Orionis.

◀ Leo is one of the most ancient constellations. Its brightest star, Regulus, is a Latin name meaning "Little King" as this was one of four Bablylonian "Royal Stars." It is also called Alpha Leonis. Denebola, Beta Leonis, comes from the Arabic meaning "Lion's Tail."

ORIGINS

We owe a great deal to the ancient civilization based on Babylon, a city on the Euphrates river south of modern Baghdad, which thrived as long as 4,000 years ago. The division of the week into seven days, the circle into 360 degrees, the hour into 60 minutes, and the basis of mathematics all came from Babylon. Some of the earliest records of the constellations come from Babylon, but their true origin may date from thousands of years before that. By 700 BC Babylonian astronomers knew about the cycles of the Sun and Moon, and could predict eclipses to within a couple of hours.

This Mesopotamian boundary ▶ stone, dating from about 1125–1100 BC, shows not only depictions of the Sun, Moon, and Venus at the top, but also illustrations of a lion and scorpion, which are still two of the best-known constellation figures.

THE SOLAR SYSTEM

Astronomers believe that the Solar System, which consists of the Sun, eight major planets, numerous moons, and millions of smaller bodies and comets, formed some 4,650 million years ago out of a cloud of gas and dust. Everything orbits around the Sun, the source of virtually all the light and heat within the Solar System. The Moon and planets shine only because they reflect the light of the Sun.

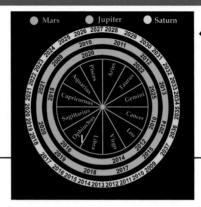

◄ Find the constellations in which oppositions of Mars, Jupiter, and Saturn will appear for each year using this planetfinder diagram. For example, in the year 2010, Mars will be at opposition in Cancer, Jupiter will be in Pisces, and Saturn will be in Leo.

HOW THE PLANETS MOVE

The planets all orbit the Sun in the same direction and in a flat plane.

Seen from Earth, the Sun always sticks to the same track (known as the ecliptic) through the sky year after year. The Moon and planets stay close to this line as well. Each body moves at a different speed, depending on its distance from the Sun and the Earth. As Johannes Kepler discovered in the seventeenth century (see page 25), the closer a planet is to the Sun, the faster it moves in its orbit. So the closest planet to the Sun, Mercury, whizzes around in just 88 days, while Neptune plods along in 165 years. The Earth takes just one year for the journey. Because Earth is the third planet out, as seen in our skies, Mercury and Venus both stick fairly close to the Sun, with Mercury only ever visible in a twilight sky.

But the other planets move along the ecliptic at varying rates, each moving from west to east. Mars moves the fastest, making its trip around the sky in less than two Earth years. Jupiter takes just under 12 years, so it moves about one twelfth of a circuit each Earth year. As there are 12 main constellations along the ecliptic (see page 27), it moves across roughly one constellation each year.

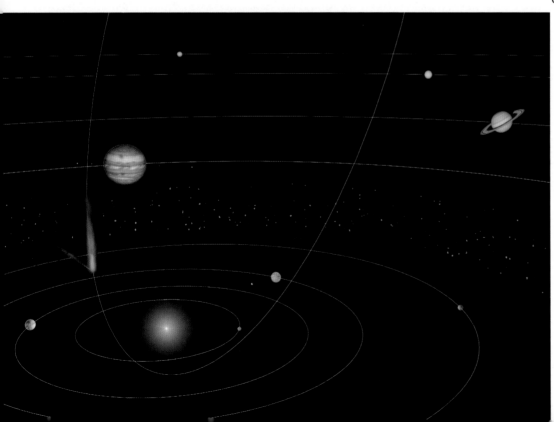

◄ The Solar System, with the Sun at center and planets Mercury, Venus, Earth, Mars, Jupiter, Saturn, Uranus and Neptune, and a comet

THE MONTHLY MOON

The Moon orbits the Earth, rather than the Sun, so it has a different set of movements. It first appears as a thin crescent (1) in the evening sky, then the illuminated portion grows over a matter of a few days until it is a half moon, at what's called first quarter (2), around 90° of sky away from the Sun. After seven more days it is full (3), and rises opposite the sun at sunset. Seven days later it is at last quarter (4), in the morning sky, and a few days after that it is a crescent again (5), in the east before sunrise. The changes in size of the Moon—its phases—are due to the changing angle of the sunlight on it.

YEARLY CYCLE

Every year or so, the planets beyond Earth are behind the Sun for a while. They then appear in the morning sky, rising before the Sun, and slowly progress into the midnight sky which is when they are closest to Earth (a point known as opposition, because they are opposite the Sun in the sky). They then move into the evening sky, getting further into the evening twilight until they are again behind the Sun.

At opposition, ▶ Jupiter (brightest object) is in the midnight sky.

Several months ▶ later, Jupiter is in the evening sky and sets shortly after the Sun.

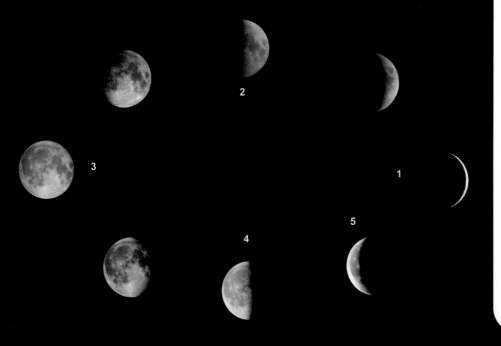

▲
The phases of the Moon in its monthly cycle

THE SUN

To us, the Sun is everything. Without it, life on Earth would be impossible. But seen from outside the Solar System, it's nothing more than an ordinary star. The reason it looks so different from the other stars is that it is so much closer to us. Light takes just eight minutes to reach us from the Sun, but over four years to reach us from even the nearest star. So imagine how many eight minutes there are in four years and you get an idea of the distance difference. The Sun has been shining steadily not just through recorded history but for billions of years—over 4.6 billion years, in fact.

OBSERVING SAFELY

The Sun is a dangerous object. You should never stare at it, and particularly not through optical aid such as binoculars, as its heat can easily cause permanent eye damage or even blindness. Special solar filters are available for use on the front of telescopes, or for observing eclipses, but only use filters specifically designed for the purpose and then only over the front and not in the eyepiece.

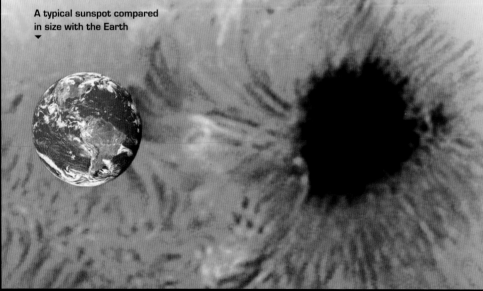

A typical sunspot compared in size with the Earth

SUNSPOTS

Using special techniques, the Sun's disk often shows spots of various sizes. These are areas where a strong magnetic field restricts the outward flow of light. However, the spots are only dark by comparison with the rest of the blindingly bright solar disk, and still emit copious amounts of light. The spots vary in number over an 11-year cycle. When they are most numerous, at what's called solar maximum, the Sun is more active in all ways, and often unleashes particle streams towards Earth. These interact with Earth's upper atmosphere to produce spectacular displays of the northern or southern lights—technically called aurorae (the plural of aurora).

ASTRO FACT

The nuclear reactions within the Sun convert matter into energy at the rate of four million tons every second. So the Sun loses this amount of mass each second—but there is enough material remaining in the Sun for it to continue shining for several billions more years.

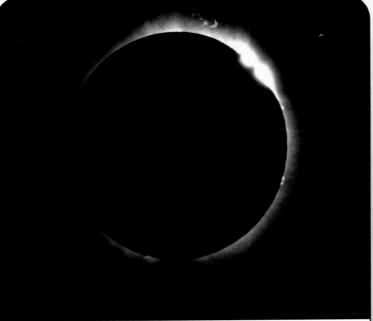

Total eclipse of the Sun

The Sun appears white when seen in its natural color ▼

ECLIPSES

Every so often, when the Moon passes directly in front of the Sun, anyone directly in the center of the Moon's shadow on the Earth may see the Sun's bright disk completely blotted out. The Sun's outer atmosphere or corona becomes visible, and eruptions of pink-glowing hydrogen gas, called prominences, may be seen at the Sun's edge. There are usually one or two such total eclipses every year, but you need to be within a few miles of the center of the Moon's shadow to see the full effect. From elsewhere, all you see is a partial eclipse.

THE MOON

Seen through binoculars or a small telescope, the Moon provides us with a whole world to explore. Its familiar features are transformed into lava plains, mountains, and craters. As the cycle of its phases progresses we see more of its surface thrown into relief. The most spectacular views of the Moon are seen along its shadow line or terminator, while around full Moon it presents just a bland face of varying light and dark patches. We are used to its face remaining the same at all times, but why doesn't the Moon rotate as the Earth does? In fact it does rotate, but in exactly the same time (29.5 days) that it takes to orbit the Earth. So we never see the far side from Earth. People often talk about the "dark side" of the Moon but in fact the far side gets as much light as the near side, and is in full sunlight when the near side is just a thin crescent.

NIGHT LIGHT

To our not-so-distant ancestors, the Moon was a crucial part of their lives. Farmers relied on the Harvest Moon to help them gather in their crops. Around September, the nearly full Moon rises at about the same time each night, providing light for harvesting.

ASTRO FACT

The Moon often looks big when it's close to the horizon but this is an optical illusion caused by comparing its size with foreground objects.

THE MOON'S FEATURES

Because it has no atmosphere, the Moon's surface has remained virtually unchanged for millions of years and it still bears the scars of bombardment by the debris left over from the formation of the Solar System billions of years ago. The largest and earliest impacts created giant basins which filled with molten lava, creating what early observers thought might be seas. They gave them fanciful names in Latin. Latin for "sea" is mare, pronounced "mah-ray", which applies to many of the features.

OBSERVING THE MOON

It's a good idea to start observing the Moon when it is a crescent and follow it through its cycle of phases. Different features become obvious as the illumination changes. Many individual craters are visible when they appear close to the terminator and mountains may throw long shadows that change length over a period of hours.

THE APOLLO MISSIONS

Between 1969 and 1972, six Apollo spacecraft landed on the Moon, each carrying two astronauts. They explored on foot and on a lunar rover up to two miles away from their craft, collecting soil samples and setting up experiments, providing information to researchers. The United States plans to revisit the Moon and set up a permanent base there after about 2018.

When the Moon is a crescent, look for Mare Crisium (1), which is about 300 miles across, and the giant craters Langrenus (2), 83 miles in diameter, and Petavius (3) 110 miles diameter.
▼

At first quarter you can see Mare Serenitatis (1) and Mare Tranquillitatis (2), where the Apollo 11 astronauts landed in 1969. The jumbled lunar highlands occupy much of the southern half.
▼

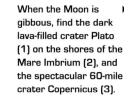

When the Moon is gibbous, find the dark lava-filled crater Plato (1) on the shores of the Mare Imbrium (2), and the spectacular 60-mile crater Copernicus (3). ▶

At full, the crater Aristarchus (1), the brightest spot on the Moon, is easy to see. Rays from the crater Tycho (2) stand out prominently. ▶

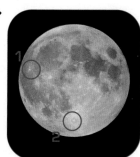

THE PLANETS

Five planets can be seen with the naked eye, and you can spot two more with binoculars. Each planet has its own characteristics, and it's often possible to recognize it just by its appearance. Planets often give themselves away by their lack of twinkling. Stars twinkle because they are points of light and our turbulent atmosphere disturbs the beam, but planets have disks and it is less easy for their light to be distorted.

MERCURY

If you spot what looks like a fairly bright star low down in the twilight after sunset or before sunrise, it may well be Mercury. Its disk is too small to be made out using binoculars. Spacecraft photos show it as being covered with craters like the Moon, though with subtle differences such as the flatness of the craters. It is virtually airless.

Mercury is only ever visible low in the twilight sky. This is Mercury's cratered landscape seen from the Messenger spacecraft.
▼

VENUS

In contrast to Mercury's shyness, Venus is the brightest of all the planets. It is also called the Evening Star or the Morning Star when it appears high up in the twilight, brilliant pure white, often against a deep blue background. Seen through a telescope, Venus displays phases like the Moon. But no details other than vague shadings are visible, because the planet is completely cloud-covered. It has a dense carbon-dioxide atmosphere and spacecraft have revealed a searingly hot, barren, volcanic landscape beneath the clouds.

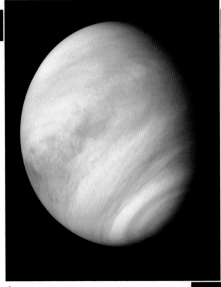
▲
The cloudy globe of Venus

Saturn, Venus, and Mercury appeared in the evening sky together in 2002.
▼

MARS

Known as the Red Planet, Mars is more a salmon-pink color. There are signs that water has flowed on its cold surface in the not-too-distant past, and there is a chance that primitive life may exist below the surface. The atmosphere consists of carbon diooxide.

◀ Mars seen with the Hubble Space Telescope

SATURN

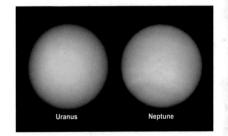

Everyone has heard of the rings of Saturn. With binoculars magnifying 10 times or more you may notice that the planet has a rather flattened appearance. A small telescope magnifying about 30 times will show the rings clearly. Saturn is gaseous and noticeably yellowish in the sky. Its rings are composed of millions of tiny chunks of ice.

JUPITER

Much more distant than Mars, Jupiter is such a giant planet that its disk is visible with binoculars, though you need a telescope to see it clearly. Jupiter has a gaseous body, so the markings are actually the tops of the clouds which change over time. Binoculars will reveal up to four of its largest moons. Over a period of hours, you may notice changes in position as they orbit the planet.

Jupiter seen from the Cassini spacecraft. The shadow of one of its moons is visible on the planet.
▼

URANUS AND NEPTUNE

Distant Uranus is on the verge of naked-eye visibility, but you would need a star chart and accurate positions to be able to distinguish it from the stars. It appears bluish through a telescope. Neptune is fainter still. Both planets are composed of ice and compressed liquid.

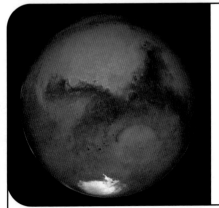
Uranus   Neptune

COMETS

Of the thousands of comets in the Solar System, few are bright enough to be easily visible. Comets are icy bodies that come in from the outer Solar System. The Sun's heat causes their ice to melt, releasing dust and gas which forms a haze around the body and possibly a tail which in some cases can be spectacular.

◀ Comet Hyakutake appeared in 1996.

BEYOND THE SOLAR SYSTEM

Stars are born from nebulae such as this, after blobs of gas condense under the pull of gravity.

A STAR IS BORN

Stars form from clouds of hydrogen and helium gas, the basic material of the universe. The gas condenses under the pull of gravity, heating up at its center until it is so hot that nuclear reactions begin. The more massive a star happens to be when it forms, the brighter it shines but the more quickly it evolves. A Sun-sized star shines normally for about 10 billion years while the most massive stars may shine for only 10 million years.

ASTRO FACT
The least massive red dwarfs stars can shine for hundreds of billions of years.

The Sun with its family of planets is just one of more than a hundred million stars in the galaxy we call the Milky Way. To see what a galaxy is you really have to look beyond the Milky Way at other galaxies. We see millions of these collections of stars stretching away into the distance. Each galaxy consists of millions of stars, so distant that all we see is haze of light.

Life cycle of a star (clockwise from top left): starbirth nebula; normal star; red giant; planetary nebula; white dwarf

At some point in its life a star runs low on its hydrogen fuel. Most stars now swell to many times their diameter but with a much lower temperature, becoming red giants. What happens next depends on the star's mass. Usually, the outer layers of the star are thrown off, forming what's called a planetary nebula surrounding the star, which is now a tiny and dense object called a white dwarf. But very massive stars explode violently as supernovae, the result being an even more dense neutron star. These may be detectable by radio astronomers as pulsars.

TYPES OF GALAXY

Spiral galaxies such as the Milky Way are beautiful structures, but the majority of galaxies are the less spectacular elliptical galaxies, which simply get brighter as you go toward the center. There are also irregular galaxies, with no definite shape. Many galaxies exist in clusters, and collisions and mergers between them are common, though they take place over billions of years. When spiral or irregular galaxies merge, there may be a burst of star formation as their gas clouds combine, but the result is usually an elliptical galaxy.

◄ An elliptical galaxy (lower left), an irregular galaxy (center), and a spiral galaxy (upper right), photographed by the Hubble Space Telescope.

THE MILKY WAY

As we are inside our own galaxy, we see it stretching all the way around the sky. The ancients called this band of light the Milky Way, and now we call it the Milky Way Galaxy. The Sun lies about two-thirds of the way from the center, so the Milky Way we see in the sky appears brighter in that direction, which lies in Sagittarius. But there are dense clouds of gas and dust between us and the center, so we can't see it directly. The dust clouds are clearly visible from country sites as a dark band, the Great Rift, along the line of the Milky Way stretching from Cygnus down to Sagittarius.

Artwork of the Milky Way seen from outside

HOW ASTRONOMERS OBSERVE

How can astronomers possibly know all the things they know—such as the distances of stars and galaxies, what stars are made of, and the age of the universe—when they can't visit these places? Almost everything we know is worked out just by looking at the objects and piecing together clues as a detective would. And like Sherlock Holmes, astronomers use magnifying glasses to give them a clearer view, except that they use giant telescopes instead.

Astronomers at work in an observatory.

OBSERVATORIES

Telescopes these days are generally located on top of mountains in remote locations. The aim is to get into clean and steady air, because the lower part of our atmosphere is often unsteady and murky. Locations close to oceans with cold currents are favored, as the cold air keeps the cloud closer to the ground. It's also essential to keep away from the lights of cities, which cause "light pollution" in the sky.

All large telescopes use dished mirrors to focus the light from faint objects. The larger the mirror, the fainter the light it can gather and the better the image quality. The mirror sizes are always quoted in meters these days. The largest telescopes have mirrors 10 or 11 meters across—about the same as the width of a tennis court. It's hard to make single mirrors this size, so they are usually made from smaller segments. There are plans for even larger telescopes in the future. Telescopes are effectively digital cameras attached to giant telephoto lenses. They are designed to take photographs with long exposure times, which requires mountings that track the sky very accurately.

The Very Large ▶ Telescope at Paranal, Chile, consists of four 8-meter telescopes, each in its own enclosure.

SPACE OBSERVATORIES

There are two advantages of putting telescopes in space. Optical telescopes in space, such as the Hubble Space Telescope (see page 45), are not affected by the atmosphere. And space observatories can observe wavelengths that can't penetrate the atmosphere at all, such as infrared, ultraviolet, X-rays, and gamma rays. As with radio waves, observations made at different wavelengths reveal different characteristics of objects.

RADIOTELESCOPES

Telescopes these days are generally located on top of mountains in remote areas. Many astronomical objects emit radio waves as well as light, and astronomers can discover a great deal about the processes going on by picking these up with giant radio dishes—essentially the same as domestic satellite dishes. Radio waves are not as badly affected by the atmosphere as light, so radiotelescopes can be located anywhere, though country sites away from sources of radio interference and air lanes are preferred.

The Chandra Space Observatory detects ▶ X-rays from the stars.

The 76-meter (250-foot) radiotelescope at Jodrell Bank, UK, has been observing from a site near Manchester since 1957.
▼

SPECTROSCOPY

▲ Spectrograms of a young, hot star (top) and a cool, red star (bottom)

As well as photography, one of the most important tools of the astronomer is spectroscopy. Many observations are not direct photographs, but spectrograms. In these, light is split up into its component wavelengths. In the case of starlight, for example, gases in the atmospheres of stars absorb particular wavelengths that reveal exactly which gases are present. Movements of the star alter the wavelength, allowing astronomers to measure the speed of a star's orbit around another star, or around the galaxy.

NORTH POLAR SKY

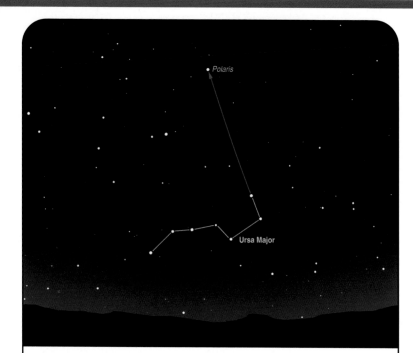

Unlike the rest of the sky, the part around the north celestial pole is visible all night, but all that changes is its orientation. The center of the north polar sky map is always the same angle above your horizon as your latitude. From North America and Europe, the Big Dipper and Cassiopeia are always visible, which will help you find the other constellations. The two are on opposite sides of the Pole Star, so when one is high in the sky, the other one is low down.

THE POLE STAR

Everyone has heard of the Pole Star (also known as Polaris or the North Star). Probably many people think it must be the brightest star in the sky. But it is not particularly bright, and its claim to fame lies in its position—by chance, it is close to the north celestial pole, so it remains close to one spot in the sky. When Europeans were first embarking on voyages of discovery, with no real navigational tools, even a glimpse of the Pole Star could tell a sailor which direction was north, and his approximate latitude. Find the Pole Star by starting from the Big Dipper. Follow the line of the two right-hand stars of the Dipper and you eventually come to a star of similar brightness as those of the Dipper. This is Polaris.

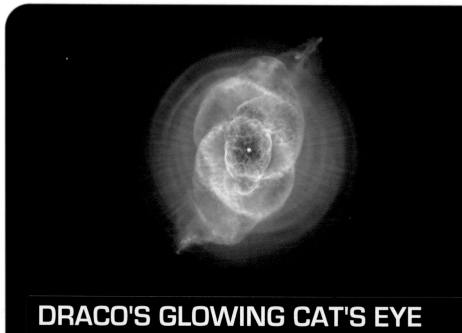

DRACO'S GLOWING CAT'S EYE

Winding its way around much of the Little Bear is a great dragon—the constellation of Draco. There are no deep-sky objects visible with binoculars, but a telescope will show a small bluish spot if you look in exactly the right place: the Cat's Eye Nebula, also known as NGC 6543. The Hubble Space Telescope's shot (above) of this shows a fantastic swirl of intricate wreaths of gas, thrown off by this dying star during its last stages of life.

RED STAR IN CEPHEUS

King Cepheus was the husband of Cassiopeia, and he sits by her in the sky. He is not as well known as his wife, partly because his star pattern is less obvious and most of his stars are fainter. One interesting star in Cepheus is Mu Cephei, famous for being one of the reddest stars that is easily visible. Take a look through binoculars, but don't expect to see something as red as a traffic light. It's no redder than a 100-watt light bulb, but its color does stand out against the others.

VIEWING THE MAP

To view this map properly, first turn the page so that the month when you are observing is at the bottom. This is the view you would get looking north at midnight on the date in question. Then turn it counterclockwise by one month for every two hours earlier. The map shows the sky from latitude 42°N. From other latitudes the horizon will cut across the bottom of the map. The farther south you are, the higher it will cut across the map until at the equator it goes right through the middle. From the southern hemisphere you will only see some of the stars for a few hours each night as they climb over your northern horizon.

Farther south than latitude ▶ 42°N, the horizon will cut off part of the map as shown.

The red star Mu Cephei (top left) lies close to a large nebula known as IC 1396, which, despite its size, is not visible to the naked eye.

◀ Map tips
The wheel shows the sky at midnight when held with the month at the bottom. Turn it one month earlier for every two hours earlier than midnight. For example, for April at 9 pm, hold it with February–March at the bottom.

21

PEGASUS AND ANDROMEDA

The Andromeda Galaxy as seen in a long-exposure photograph.

At this time of year there are few bright stars around, but instead there is one of the best signposts in the sky—the Square of Pegasus. The Square is easy to find, though it is a lazy square a bit fainter and bigger than you might imagine. Its sides act as pointers to other constellations, notably Andromeda. It actually shares the star at its northeastern corner with Andromeda. Its vertical sides point south to Cetus and to the bright star Fomalhaut, while its diagonals point to Pisces and Aquarius.

BEAUTIFUL ANDROMEDA'S GALAXY

The beautiful princess Andromeda is part of myths that involve her rescue by Perseus from the sea monster Cetus, way down to the south, as described on page 24. The constellation itself is somewhat plain—three brightish stars in a widely spaced line, including one member of the Square of Pegasus; one less bright; and a handful of others which are fairly inconsequential. But one feature of Andromeda sets it apart from all other constellations. This part of the sky is home to our nearest large galaxy, the Andromeda Galaxy, also known as M31. Like the Milky Way Galaxy, it is a member of a small collection of galaxies known as the Local Group, with M33 in Triangulum as the next largest after ourselves and M31. The Andromeda Galaxy is about 2.5 million light-years away, and for most people is the most distant object that they can see with the naked eye, though a few can spot M33 as well. It is the largest member of the Local Group, containing up to five times as many stars as our own galaxy.

FINDING ANDROMEDA'S GALAXY

To find M31, locate the line of three stars in Andromeda and the not-so-bright one, and, starting from the Square of Pegasus count two along, then turn north and count a further two stars. You should come to a distinctly oval blur. This little fuzz is actually a mighty galaxy like our own Milky Way, unimaginable in true size, and consisting of perhaps a trillion stars. And just such a fuzz is what we look like to them. There must be people in that galaxy saying just the same about us—even if the chances of intelligent life forming on a planet are a million to one, there must still be eyes gazing up at us. Yet the light you see tonight left the Andromeda Galaxy about 2.5 million years ago, so those eyes, and probably even their civilizations, are now long dead.

The Pinwheel Galaxy, M33, in Triangulum, is a face-on spiral galaxy with a lower surface brightness than M31. Some people can see it with the naked eye, making it the most distant object normally visible, at 2.8 million light-years.

Globular cluster M15 in Pegasus as it appears through a large telescope. The star above it is visible using binoculars.

PEGASUS

Pegasus is a winged horse, steed of the Greek hero Bellerophon, who jointly undertook great deeds. But, sadly, only the front half of the horse is shown in the stars, and to add insult to injury the poor creature is upside down, in the northern hemisphere at least. Pegasus contains just one object easily seen in binoculars—a globular cluster, M15. This is not far from Enif, the star which marks the horse's nose. It appears as a circular haze, brighter at the center, but you need a medium-sized telescope to see individual stars.

TRIANGULUM

This small constellation is home to another nearby galaxy—the Pinwheel Galaxy, M33. It can be hard to see but to find it, retrace your route to find the Andromeda Galaxy and, instead of turning north, turn south the same distance from the main line of stars.

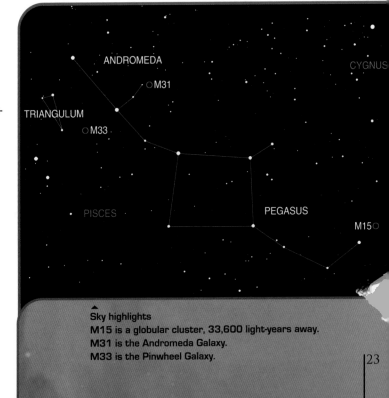

Sky highlights
M15 is a globular cluster, 33,600 light-years away.
M31 is the Andromeda Galaxy.
M33 is the Pinwheel Galaxy.

CASSIOPEIA AND PERSEUS

The "W" shape of Cassiopeia is one of the most easily recognized patterns in the whole sky. It swings around the Pole Star exactly opposite the Big Dipper. To its east lies Perseus—less obvious as a pattern, but still easily spotted as its main stars are of similar brightness to those of Cassiopeia. It has a line of three or four stars joined by another line at an angle—a sort of lazy or italic "T".

THE LEGEND OF CASSIOPEIA

Several of the constellations in this part of the sky are related to one another by mythology. Cassiopeia, wife of King Cepheus, is a vain queen with a beautiful daughter, Andromeda. To punish her mother's vanity, Andromeda is chained to rocks where she will be eaten by the fierce sea monster Cetus. Along comes the hero Perseus, who previously killed the gorgon Medusa—and of course saves her.

VIEWING CASSIOPEIA

Cassiopeia lies in the northern Milky Way, which is crowded with stars as seen through binoculars. You will spot little knots and lines of stars, and there are several richer clusters, the most obvious being NGC 663, which is just to one side of the line joining the two easternmost stars of the "W".

Star atlas version of Cassiopeia

The Double Cluster in Perseus under perfect conditions, when the whole view is full of stars.

PERSEUS THE HERO

Perseus is a glittering constellation, particularly when viewed with binoculars, because around his brightest star, Mirphak, is a scatter of fainter stars in an obvious "S" shape. This is a wide cluster of stars, just as attractive as anything visible with a telescope. But an even more dazzling sight, one of the true showpieces of the sky, lies nearby. Scan the sky between Perseus and Cassiopeia and you will find a Double Cluster, visible in even poor skies but stunning in a dark sky. You can spot them with the naked eye, but you need binoculars or a telescope to turn the hazy spot into real stars.

HOW A STAR CHANGED EVERYTHING

In 1572 the Danish astronomer Tycho Brahe looked up at Cassiopeia and to his amazement saw a brilliant star where none had been previously. At that time, the stars were thought to be attached to crystal spheres that couldn't change. Yet here was an obvious "flaw" in the firmament. We now know that it was a rare supernova—an exploding star. He went on to measure the positions of the stars and planets very precisely (at a time before telescopes were invented), allowing his pupil Johannes Kepler to investigate the movements of the planets very carefully.

Kepler came up with a radical conclusion. Instead of the planets going around the Earth, thought to be the center of the Universe, the Earth and the other planets orbit the Sun. They don't orbit in circles, as Copernicus had suggested in 1543, but in ellipses—slightly flattened circles—and move faster when closer to the Sun than when farther away. Kepler's Laws of planetary motion are still at the heart of our understanding of the solar system.

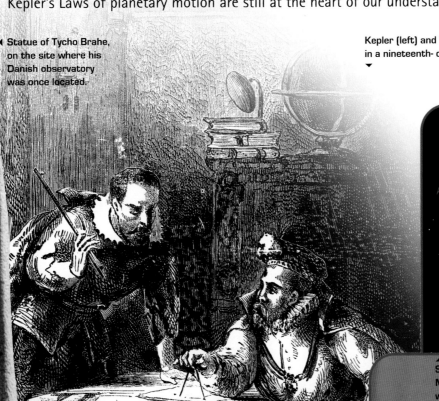

◀ Statue of Tycho Brahe, on the site where his Danish observatory was once located.

Kepler (left) and Tycho as depicted in a nineteenth- century engraving.
▼

CASSIOPEIA
M52
AURIGA
NGC 663
NGC 869
NGC 884
Mirphak
PERSEUS
M34
ANDROMEDA

Sky highlights
M34, M52, and NGC 663 are star clusters visible with binoculars. NGC 869 and NGC 884 constitute the Double Cluster, visible with the naked eye.

25

AQUARIUS AND CAPRICORNUS

Despite being well-known zodiacal constellations, Aquarius and Capricornus have no bright stars. To find Aquarius, take a diagonal southwestward across the Square of Pegasus and you end up not far from one of the main stars in Aquarius, Sadalmelik. The best route to Capricornus is to follow the line of three stars that contains Altair southeastward until you come to a pair of stars on the same line which mark the western end of the constellation.

AQUARIUS

These are watery regions of the sky. Aquarius is the Water-Carrier, nearby Capricornus is the Sea-Goat, next door is Cetus, the Sea Monster—and it's more than coincidence. In times gone by, when the Middle Eastern peoples were making up star stories to tell around the campfire, the Sun was in this part of the sky during the rainy season, so it seemed there was a link between these constellations and water. Aquarius is doing his bit, keeping the oceans full using his ever-full water jar.

The stars of Aquarius with the constellation figure superimposed

CAPRICORNUS

Note that this is the astronomical name for the constellation, not Capricorn, which is the astrologers' sign. It's even less striking than Aquarius, and its main object of interest is the star Alpha Capricorni or Algedi. This is a well-known naked-eye double star: it consists of two stars of similar brightness, close together in the sky. You should be able to distinguish the two stars with average eyesight. They are actually unrelated stars, with the brighter one being 109 light-years away and the fainter one 687 light-years away.

The constellations of the Zodiac stretch right around the heavens.

ARIES   PISCES   AQUARIUS   CAPRICORNUS   SAGITTARIUS   SCORPIUS   LIBRA   VIRGO   LEO   CANCER   GEMINI   TAURUS

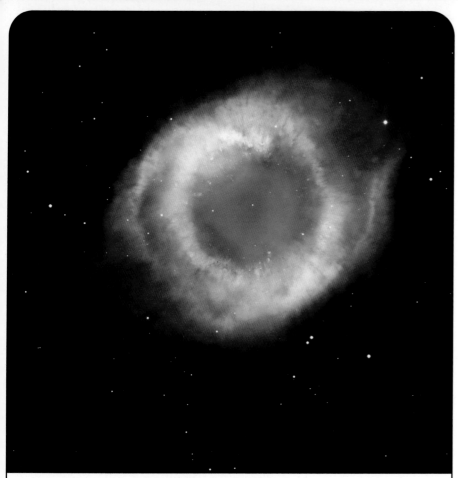

THE ZODIAC AND ASTROLOGY

Why are faint constellations such as Aquarius and Capricornus so well known? The answer lies more than 3,000 years ago in Babylonian astrology. In an attempt to relate happenings on Earth to the movements of the heavens, astrologers divided the path of the Sun, Moon, and planets through the sky into 12 parts. But the actual constellation patterns do not provide 12 neat groups of equal size, and some are particularly poor in stars. The word zodiac comes from a Greek term, "circle of animals," as the majority of the constellations of the zodiac represent animals.

What's called "newspaper astrology" refers largely to the positions of the bodies of the Solar System against the background of these "signs of the Zodiac." It's fair to say that the vast majority of astronomers believe that astrology is bunk!

◄ The Hubble Space Telescope photo of the Helix Nebula shows dramatic shells of gas surrounding a faint central star. The shells appear like a coil or helix, giving the nebula its name.

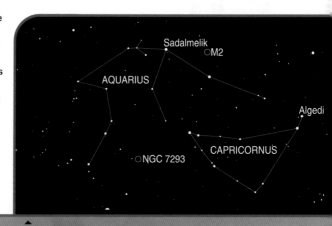

THE HELIX NEBULA

There are no spectacular binocular objects in Aquarius, but it is home to the Helix Nebula. At around 700 light-years, this is said to be the closest planetary nebula to Earth, and it's a spectacular and colorful ring in the photos, but try to find it in anything but a really good, dark sky with binoculars and you'll be disappointed. It's a very faint ring, appearing about one-third the size of the full Moon. The farther south you are, the easier it is to find.

Sky highlights
Algedi consists of two stars, though the pair are unrelated and are at different distances. M2 is a globular cluster 37,500 light-years away.

27

ARIES, PISCES, AND CETUS

A nineteenth-century depiction of Aries ▼

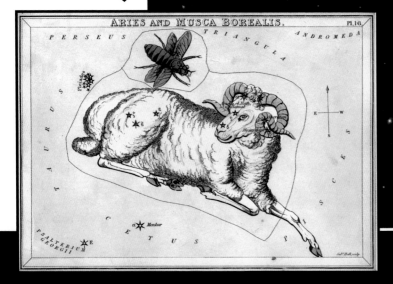

Like several other well-known constellations of the zodiac, Aries and Pisces are not blessed with very bright stars. Aries is the easiest to spot, with two brightish stars and a fainter one, to the east of the Square of Pegasus. Pisces is really only visible in dark skies, and consists of two straggling lines of stars to the east and south of the Square.

Main stars of Aries ▶

ARIES, PISCES, AND CETUS

The pattern of Aries, the Ram, is recognizable only because there are no other bright stars nearby. It consists of two main stars, named Hamal and Sheratan, accompanied by a third, known as Mesartim or just as Gamma. The three make a distinctive trio, even though Gamma is not as bright as a couple of outlying stars in the constellation.

The ram in question is a particularly famous one—the same ram that provided the Golden Fleece that was the subject of the quest of Jason and the Argonauts. In Ancient Greek times, Aries was the constellation in which the Sun crossed from the southern to the northern hemispheres, marking the start of spring. These days, due to a slow wobble of the Earth's axis known as "precession", the Sun is in Pisces when it does this, but the point is still occasionally referred to as the First Point of Aries.

There are no binocular objects in Aries, though Gamma is a favorite double star with amateur astronomers, consisting of two well-separated white stars.

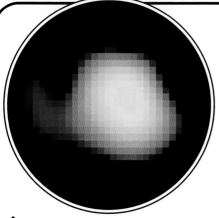

CETUS

This Sea Monster features in the tale of Perseus and Andromeda, as the one deprived of its meal of the beautiful princess by the heroism of Perseus. It's a large, sprawling constellation as you would imagine, with a couple of reasonably bright stars most of the time, the brightest being Deneb Kaitos or Diphda, which lies well to the south of the eastern edge of the Square of Pegasus.

A close-up of Mira photographed by the Hubble Space Telescope.

MIRA THE WONDER STAR

Occasionally there is a brighter star in Cetus. Most of the time it is dim, if not invisible to the naked eye, but about every 330 days it brightens for a few weeks to become one of the brightest stars in the constellation. It was the first star of variable brightness to be noticed, the discovery being made by Dutch astronomer David Fabricius in 1596. It was named Mira, meaning "Wonderful", for its behavior. Mira is a red giant star of huge proportions. Observations show that Mira has trouble maintaining its shape and is subject to unruly bulges.

PISCES, THE FISH

We often have to remember that the ancients who named the constellations enjoyed much darker skies than most of us do these days. The two lines of stars that mark the two fish are virtually invisible from suburban locations. Actually the lines mark strings that tie each fish, which are indicated by groups of stars at their ends. The fish below the Square of Pegasus is easiest to see, as it consists of a rough circle of stars known as the Circlet.

ASTRO FACT

Pisces is home to the galaxy M74, a spiral galaxy. Though quite hard to see with a small telescope, it's well-known because of its classic spiral shape—often referred to as a "Grand Design" spiral. It strongly resembles the way we believe our own Milky Way would look from outside.

Galaxy M74 ▶

Sky highlights
The Circlet is indicated on the map immediately to the south of the Square of Pegasus. M74 is a galaxy about 32 million light-years away.

ORION

THE HUNTER OF GREEK MYTHOLOGY

Looking at the stars of Orion it's not too hard to imagine the fearless Hunter, holding his shield aloft, doing battle against the raging bull, Taurus. For once, the stars fit in fairly well with the figure they are meant to show. To add to the spectacle, Orion is the most brilliant constellation for its number of bright stars. Although Orion the Hunter features in Greek mythology, the bull does not. Orion probably predates the Ancient Greeks by a few thousand years, and is believed to originate with the Sumerian civilization in what is now Iraq. He is the classic hero, about to slay the bull, and with his faithful dog by his side.

It's no coincidence that the stars of Orion are such a spectacle. The whole area is the nearest major starbirth region to Earth. Many of the stars we see are young, hot, and blue, and are all at roughly the same distance, around 1,300 light-years.

◄ The stars of Orion

After the Big Dipper or Southern Cross, Orion is the one constellation that many people know. It's very distinctive, and easy to find in the skies from November to March, high in mid sky. The line of three stars that mark Orion's belt are surrounded by a quadrilateral of four others, two of which are among the 10 brightest in the sky. It is our Signpost constellation for January to March skies, and straddles the celestial equator so it is equally visible from northern and southern hemispheres.

BETELGEUSE

The star that marks Orion's shoulder is noticeably more orange than the others, as it's a red supergiant star. Betelgeuse is one of the few stars large enough and close enough that it shows a measurable actual disk, though you need the Hubble Space Telescope to see it! If Betelgeuse were in the Solar System, Jupiter might find itself on the outer edges of the star's atmosphere.

◄ The red supergiant star Betelgeuse. The star is 427 light-years away–about one-third the distance of the other stars in Orion.

HORSEHEAD NEBULA

As well as the Orion Nebula there are several others in the area. The best known is the Horsehead—actually a region of dark dusty gas silhouetted by thinner glowing gas beyond. It's very hard to see—you need perfect skies and a good telescope, and even then the shape of the horse's head is hard to make out—so the best way to enjoy it is in its photographs. Notice how the stars in the pink area are much more numerous than in the dark area. This is because we are seeing through the thin gas to more numerous background stars. There are just a few foreground stars between us and the Horsehead.

Horsehead Nebula in Orion ▶

ORION NEBULA

Starbirth regions are associated with great clouds of gas and dust, and we can see the evidence in the Orion Nebula, also known as M42. To find it, look directly below the three stars on Orion's belt for a line of fainter stars, running north-south. The center of this line is misty, particularly when viewed through binoculars in a dark sky. This is the Orion Nebula. Within it, new stars are being born—though slowly by human standards, so don't expect to see one light up as you watch. It's just the brightest part of a cloud of dark gas that covers almost the entire constellation. Infrared studies reveal many more stars that are hidden from our view.

To the eye, the Orion Nebula just looks gray, but in photos it shows pink. The pink color is the natural color of hydrogen gas that is made to fluoresce by ultraviolet light from nearby hot stars.

Horsehead and nearby Flame Nebula, a mix of bright and dark gases ▶

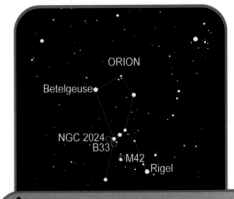

Sky highlights
M42 is the Orion Nebula, about 1,300 light-years away. NGC 2024 is the Flame Nebula, while B33 is the dark nebula known as the Horsehead.

31

AURIGA

Lying immediately to the north of Orion, Auriga is a pentagon of stars with a brilliant star, Capella, at its apex. As seen from North America and Europe, Capella is almost overhead during the winter months, and is one of the brightest stars in the sky.

AURIGA'S JEWELS

Auriga

In Auriga, three exquisite clusters in a line are visible with the naked eye in dark skies. Each is subtly different. The easternmost, M37, is by far the richest in stars, while the middle one, M36, is smaller. The westernmost, M38, is larger but with fainter stars. All three lie at roughly the same distance, between 4,000 and 4,400 light-years.

ASTRO FACT

Capella is a noticeably yellowish star, consisting of two separate but very close stars that are both becoming red giants over millions of years. The pair are 42 light-years from the Sun.

THE CHARIOTEER

Although Auriga is less well-known than Orion, it shares the same region of sky and is one of the major constellations. Although most people see a pentagon of stars, which is how the classical representations show the constellation, strictly speaking the southernmost star, known as El Nath, is really part of Taurus and marks one of the bull's horns.

There are several charioteers called Auriga in Greek myths, and which one of several he represents depends on which writer you read. One notable feature is that he carries with him through the sky a goat and her two kids. The goat itself is marked by Capella, a name which translates as "she-goat", while the two kids, known as Haedi, are the southerly two of the triangle of stars adjacent to the star.

The northern Milky Way runs through Auriga, so it is rich with clouds of faint stars that make for great viewing with binoculars. As you sweep through the area you can't miss three bright clusters, known as M36, M37, and M38.

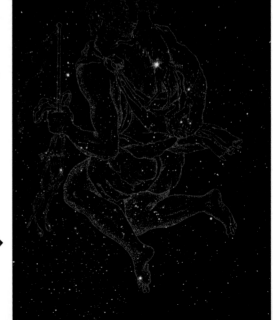

The charioteer Auriga, tirelessly ▶ carrying a goat and her two kids through the heavens.

FLAMING STAR NEBULA

Not far from M38 is a favorite nebula for sky photographers, known as the Flaming Star Nebula. As well as making a pretty sight, there is a story behind it. At the center of the nebula is a star known as AE Aurigae, which provides the ultraviolet light that illuminates the whole nebula. This star is an escapee from the region of the Orion Nebula. It was once the companion of another star that exploded in a supernova. Released from its ties, AE Aurigae hurtled across space to end up here, where it is now illuminating the Flaming Star Nebula as it passes by.

USING BINOCULARS

Binoculars are an ideal means of getting to know the sky as they show fainter stars and objects than you can see with the eye alone. While small portable binoculars are useful, astronomers prefer sizes such as 10 x 50, where 10 is the magnification and 50 is the diameter of the main lenses in millimeters. Make sure you adjust the binoculars properly before using them. First, use the focusing wheel to focus while looking through the fixed eyepiece only (usually the left half), then focus the adjustable eyepiece only, without touching the main focus wheel. Also, adjust the width carefully to the distance between your eyes.

Focusing using the ▶
eyepiece adjuster

AURIGA

Capella

M38
M36
M37
El Nath

Sky highlights
The star immediately to the lower right of Capella, Epsilon Aurigae, undergoes a year-long dimming every 27 years as a dark companion object eclipses it. Eclipses occur in 2009–11 and 2036–8.

GEMINI AND CANIS MINOR

Find Gemini by starting from the signpost constellation of Orion. Take a line from Rigel through Betelgeuse and you'll spot the two bright stars of Gemini. South of these, and roughly level with Betelgeuse, is a single bright star, Procyon, in Canis Minor. Farther south still and you get to the scattered stars of the really faint Monoceros.

The Eskimo Nebula, ▶ photographed by the Hubble Space Telescope. It gets its name from the fur hood effect of the surrounding shell of material.

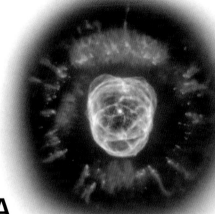

▲ Gemini, with Castor and Pollux (left) and Alhena (right)

ESKIMO NEBULA

This object in Gemini, called the Eskimo Nebula, is a favorite of amateur astronomers, though it's not visible with binoculars. It's quite easy to find with a medium-sized telescope, but requires a magnification of around 50 because it looks quite starlike at lower magnifications. But it takes a photo with a large telescope to bring out the likeness to a head surrounded by a fur hood. It's a planetary nebula, and the photo shows at its center the white dwarf star which threw off the shells of gas.

GEMINI, THE HEAVENLY TWINS

You might think before you saw them that the pair of stars known as the Heavenly Twins would be close together and an exact pair. Actually, they are neither especially close, nor are they evenly matched, either in brightness or in color, but oddly enough there are not that many pairs of bright stars in the sky which are more of a boxed set.

The names of these twin stars are Castor and Pollux. In mythology they were the offspring of Leda, Queen of Sparta, but these twins had different fathers. One was the famous Zeus, king of the gods, while the other was Leda's rightful husband, King Tyndareus.

ASTRO FACT

Gemini consists of two rough lines of stars, one for each twin, with their feet closest to Orion. Close to Castor's left foot is a star cluster, M35, easily seen with binoculars. It lies close to the ecliptic, so a planet may sometimes be seen apparently caught among its stars.

MONOCEROS

Although Monoceros, the Unicorn, is poor in stars it has a good measure of other objects. In a good, dark sky with binoculars you can spot several pretty clusters, particularly the open cluster M50, though a small telescope is needed to show it well.

CANIS MINOR

The only point of interest in Canis Minor, the Lesser Dog, is the bright star Procyon. It's a small constellation between Gemini and Monoceros, and is close to the Milky Way. Procyon is so called because from the latitude of Greece it rises just before the Dog Star, Sirius, itself. The name means "before the dog."

ROSETTE NEBULA

The Rosette Nebula is one of the most popular images in astronomy books, and it shows up well even on wide-field photos of the area, yet visually it's virtually invisible because its red light is not easily seen by eye. The cluster of stars at its center can be seen with binoculars, though rather disappointingly, but don't expect to see the delicate wreaths of light that give the nebula its name. It is a region of hydrogen gas from which stars, probably those in the central cluster, have been born.

▲ The Rosette Nebula, with the cluster NGC 2244 at its center. It lies about 5,500 light-years away from us.

Sky highlights
M35 is a star cluster, while NGC 2444 is a star cluster surrounded by the Rosette Nebula. NGC 2392 is the Eskimo Nebula.

CANIS MAJOR AND PUPPIS

Marked by the brightest star in the night sky, Canis Major is easy to spot using Orion's Belt as a signpost. Follow the three Belt stars southeastward and you come to Sirius, a brilliant white star. Several other bright stars of Canis Major form a very simple stick figure of a dog, with the stars of Puppis farther south.

The stars of Canis Major, with Sirius above center

THE GREAT DOG—Canis Major

In Greek myths, the Great Dog is often said to be Laelaps, the swiftest dog ever—just the dog that you would expect to follow Orion, the hunter. He crops up in many different legends. But historians believe that it's Sirius, the Dog Star, that gave its name to the constellation rather than the star being named after the myths. The reason why it is called the Dog Star is unknown—it seems to be a very ancient connection. Sirius was a very important star to the Egyptians, and its name persists in modern language. The hot days of summer are known as Dog Days—because during summer in the northern hemisphere, Sirius is in the sky at the same time as the Sun, supposedly adding its rays and heat to that of the Sun.

Just 4° south of Sirius lies a bright cluster, M41. It's well worth a look in binoculars, and is easy to find—with Sirius at one edge of the field of view, you will find M41 just beyond the opposite edge. This cluster is about 2,300 light-years away from us, so if Sirius were a member of this cluster it would hardly be visible.

The cluster M41 ▶

ASTRO FACT

The reason why Sirius is such a bright star is that it is very close to us, astronomically speaking, at just 8.6 light-years, and it is also some 20 times brighter than the Sun. It dominates our celestial neighborhood. The other major stars of Canis Major are much more distant and even brighter in their own right, putting Sirius to shame. Adhara, for example, is about 430 light-years away and is about 3,500 times as bright as the Sun.

Artist's impression of Sirius and Sirius B closeup

SIRIUS AND THE EGYPTIANS

To the Ancient Egyptians, the appearance of Sirius just before sunrise in July was a sign that the most important event of the year—the annual flooding of the Nile—was about to take place. This was a sign in the sky that everyone in the fields could recognize, and was independent of the Egyptian calendar which lacked leap years and got out of step with the seasons. So Sirius was the most important star to the Egyptians, as the Nile flood brought water and fertility back to the land.

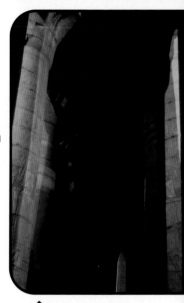

Sirius seen through the ruins of Karnak, Egypt.

SIRIUS

Sirius is a double star—like the majority of stars in the sky, in fact. However, the companion is not an ordinary star but a white dwarf, called Sirius B, or sometimes, playfully, as the Pup. It would once have been a much more massive and brighter star than its birthmate Sirius, but more massive stars evolve quicker, and in due course it blew off some of its mass as a planetary nebula and shrank down to a white dwarf. It is now only the diameter of the Earth. This means that a sugar-cube-sized piece of the star would weigh about two tons—the same as an SUV. The once-brilliant Pup is now faint, and is too close to Sirius to be seen easily.

Sirius photographed with the Hubble Space Telescope. Sirius B is the tiny dot at the 11 o'clock position, on the edge of the outer circle of light.

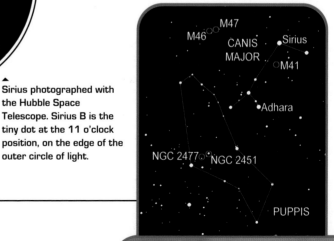

PUPPIS

Southeast of Canis Major lie the stars of Puppis, the poop deck of what was once the giant constellation of Argo Navis—the ship in which Jason and the Argonauts sailed. There are several bright clusters in Puppis, as shown on the map (right).

Star cluster sky highlights
M41 is 2,300 light-years away, with M46 at 5,400 light-years, M47 at 1,600 light-years, NGC 2451 at 850 light-years, and NGC 2477 at 4,200 light-years.

TAURUS AND THE PLEIADES

To find the stars of Taurus, begin with the three stars of the belt of Orion. They point northwest to a bright, orange star, Aldebaran, which marks the eye of the bull, Taurus. Carry on farther and you'll find the unmistakable star cluster called the Pleiades.

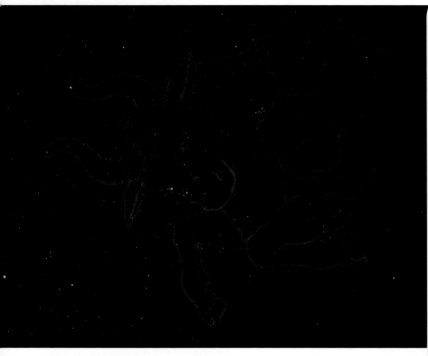

▲ Red giant star Aldebaran traditionally marks the eye of the Bull

THE CELESTIAL BULL

The stars of Taurus have reminded people of a bull for thousands of years, possibly since pre-history. A cave painting at Lascaux in France has a strong resemblance to the classical figure of the bull with the Pleiades cluster. In classical mythology, one tale relates that the bull is the king of the gods, Zeus, in one of the many disguises he adopted in order to get up close and personal with a fair maiden, in this case Europa, daughter of the king of Phoenicia.

One key feature of the constellation that makes the link to a bull is a group of stars known as the Hyades (pronounced Hy-a-deez), a V-shape of stars with Aldebaran at one tip of the V. The bull shape is completed by two stars that mark the tips of its long horns. The Hyades are a genuine cluster about 150 light-years away, though Aldebaran itself is less than half that distance at 65 light-years.

▲ Taurus

ASTRO FACT

People often wonder how astronomers can measure such vast distances, and the Hyades hold the clue. We know that they are moving in parallel paths through space fairly close to us, so careful plotting of their motions through the sky allows us to estimate their true distance. This gives us a reference set of stars with which we can compare others that look similar.

THE PLEIADES

Taurus is home to the most spectacular star cluster in the sky—the Pleiades (pronounced Ply-a-deez), also known as the Seven Sisters. In fact, there are more than seven stars in the group, but seven is a popular number and the ancients did not let the facts stand in the way of a catchy name. People with good eyes can spot well over a dozen in dark skies. Nine have names—being the seven sisters and their parents. The cluster is about 400 light-years away. Binoculars are the ideal way to view the Pleiades. There are around 100 stars in the cluster altogether. In a good sky the stars look luminous beyond their true brightness, and deep photographs show that the area is surrounded by dust. It glows blue, the color of interstellar dust, rather than pink, the color of hydrogen, as the cluster just happens to be passing through a dusty area.

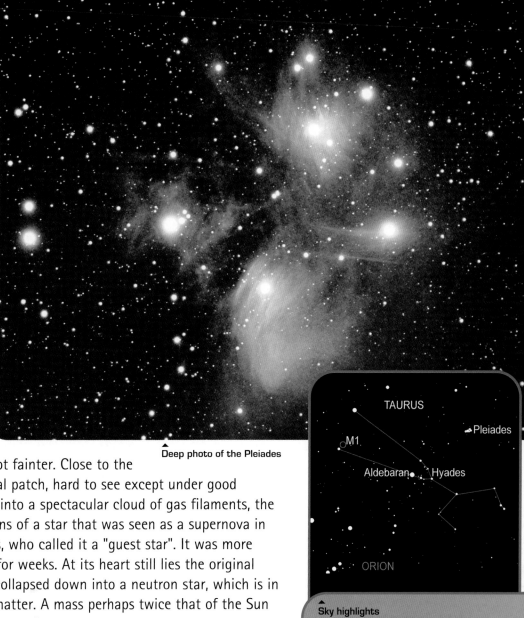

Deep photo of the Pleiades

THE CRAB NEBULA

The other famous sight in Taurus is a lot fainter. Close to the star Zeta Tauri is a small misty oval patch, hard to see except under good conditions. Photographs turn it into a spectacular cloud of gas filaments, the Crab Nebula. This is the remains of a star that was seen as a supernova in 1054 by Chinese astronomers, who called it a "guest star". It was more brilliant than any other star for weeks. At its heart still lies the original star, now a feeble relic, but collapsed down into a neutron star, which is in an incredibly dense state of matter. A mass perhaps twice that of the Sun is crushed into a sphere about 20 miles across.

◀ The Crab Nebula photographed by the Very Large Telescope in Chile

TAURUS

Pleiades

M1

Aldebaran   Hyades

ORION

Sky highlights
M1 is the Crab Nebula, 6,300 light-years away.

39

LEO AND CANCER

The oldest constellations are probably those that really do remind people of real creatures, and Leo is one. It probably dates from thousands of years ago, judging by ancient carvings (see page 7). The curved line of stars that make up the lion's mane is not bright but it's very distinctive. Some people believe that the Sphinx in Egypt is modeled on Leo, and there is a strong resemblance. The Sphinx faces east, though Leo actually rises some 30º north of this point.

▲ Leo figure

LEO THE LION

In Greek mythology this is the lion killed by Heracles—or in Latin, Hercules—as the first of his 12 labors. The lion had been particularly troublesome to the locals, but as the king of the beasts it deserves its place among the stars. To country folk in later times, the curved shape of its mane was better known as the Sickle—undoubtedly a more familiar sight than that of a lion.

The chief sights of Leo for binoculars are two galaxies, M65 and M66, lying just south of the star Chertan. They are small, so they show up best with the higher magnification instruments.

Meteors from ▶
Leo in 2002

LEONID METEORS

Leo is famous for being the apparent source, in November, of the Leonid meteors. Meteors, or shooting stars, are tiny flecks of comet dust that have spread far from the orbit of the original comet. In this case, the Earth passes through the cloud of dust around November 17 each year, with the result that the dust specks burn up in our atmosphere, giving rise to streaks of light that appear to radiate away from a particular point in the sky. The display starts as Leo rises, about 10.30 p.m. In most years there may be one every few minutes, but occasionally the Earth passes through a denser clump of dust and the numbers can rise dramatically. In 1833, and again in 1966, amazing storms of shooting stars were seen, with hundreds of meteors a second filling the sky. Other meteor showers occur regularly around 4 January (Quadrantid meteors, from Boötes), 12 August (Perseids), and 14 December (Geminids).

ASTRO FACT

The 1833 Leonid meteor shower was commemorated in the song "Stars Fell on Alabama," written over 100 years after the meteor shower occurred.

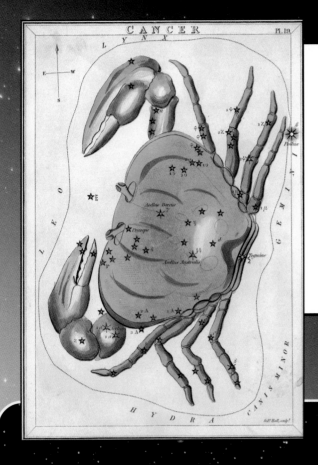

A nineteenth-century star atlas illustration of the stars of Cancer

CANCER

A small and faint constellation, virtually invisible from suburban locations, Cancer marks the final resting place of an unfortunate mythological crab that bit Hercules and was crushed underfoot as a result. But though its stars are faint, it contains a star cluster that is a jewel among clusters—the Beehive. For binocular users this is one of the best in the sky, second only to the Pleiades in its brightness. In dark skies it's easily visible with the naked eye as a haze close to a pair of stars known as the Donkeys: Asellus Borealis and Asellus Australis. For this reason, an alternative name for the Beehive Cluster is the Manger, or in Latin, Praesepe. Its catalog number is M44.

◄ A nineteenth-century star atlas
   illustration of the stars of Cancer

Beehive Cluster
▼

LEO

CANCER

Asellus Borealis
Asellus Australis
M44

Chertan

Denebola
M66 M65

Regulus

▲
Sky highlights
M44 is the Beehive Cluster or Praesepe,
577 light-years away. M65 and M66 are
galaxies, each 35 million light-years away.

URSA MAJOR AND BOÖTES

If there's one constellation that most people know, at least in the northern hemisphere, it's the Big Dipper (more properly known as Ursa Major). But where is it? In October and November it's down on the northern horizon and easy to see, but by February it's swung around high in the northeast and by May it's virtually overhead. By August it's still high but in the northwest. From most parts of the southern hemisphere it's nearly always below the horizon.

ASTRO FACT

Look at Mizar, the middle star of the Dipper's handle, and you should spot another star, Alcor, nearby. Mizar itself is a double star, though you'd need a telescope to see the two separately. Double stars are a major tool for astronomers, as they are the only way that we can judge the true masses of the stars, using Newton's Laws of Motion.

URSA MAJOR

In North America it's the Big Dipper, in Britain it's the Plough (and is shown on many a pub sign), in France it's the Casserole, but everywhere the seven main stars of Ursa Major, the Great Bear, are well-known. Many cultures regarded these stars as a bear, and in fact the Arctic itself gets its name from these stars, which constantly wheel above it. Arktos is Greek for "bear," and the region is in fact named after the constellation and not because there are polar bears there!

M81 ▶

The constellation contains two galaxies, M81 and M82. Follow the diagonal of the bowl of the Dipper to the northeast, and you should spot them, tiny but distinct. The cigar shape of M82 is very noticeable. Another well-known galaxy, the Whirlpool Galaxy, M51, is close to the end of the Dipper's handle, in the neighboring constellation of Canes Venatici (the Hunting Dogs). This was the first galaxy to be seen as a spiral, back in 1845 by Lord Rosse from Birr in Ireland, who had built what was then the largest telescope in the world.

Ursa Major and the Big Dipper

The region around Boötes as depicted in a nineteenth-century star atlas

BOÖTES

This large constellation mostly contains rather faint stars, but the brightest, Arcturus, is the fourth brightest in the night sky. Find it by following the curve of the Dipper's handle around in a large curve. Arcturus lies 37 light-years away. In the past its distance was thought to be 40 light-years, so when Chicago decided to have a World's Fair in 1933, they used its light to trigger an electric relay to open the fair—the significance being that the light was supposed to have started its journey at the time of the previous Chicago World's Fair, in 1893. Boötes—pronounced "Boo-oh-teez"—represents a herdsman, though to modern eyes it looks like a kite. The circlet of stars is Corona Borealis, the Northern Crown.

NEWTON AND GRAVITY

Sir Isaac Newton's discoveries are at the heart of much of astronomy. His genius lay in his ability to seemingly stand outside the world and see things afresh. For example, he realized that the force that pulls an apple from a tree is the same that keeps the Moon in orbit; and that objects moving in space will continue to move without being pushed, until some force acts on them. On Earth, friction soon brings things to a halt. Linking these mathematically, he came up with Laws of Motion that still enable us to calculate masses when all we know is the weight of one, and the distance between them, as in some double stars.

Woolsthorpe Manor, Lincolnshire, England, where Newton was born, with apple tree in foreground

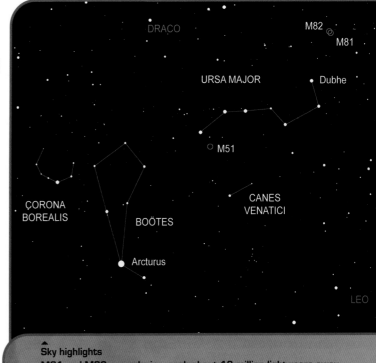

Sky highlights
M81 and M82 are galaxies, each about 12 million light-years away. They are among the easiest galaxies to view using binoculars, after the members of the Local Group. M51, the Whirlpool Galaxy, is 37 million light-years away.

VIRGO AND LIBRA

Spica is Virgo's only bright star, but in a part of the sky where there are few rivals it is easy to find, either by looking to the southeast of Leo, or by following the curve of the Big Dipper's handle around past Arcturus (see page 43). It lies at the base of a Y-shape of stars extending toward Leo, plus a few outliers. To its southwest is a trapezium of four stars. Corvus (the Crow) and to its southeast are two main stars of the rather unimpressive Libra. Immediately north of the bowl of the Y-shape is a compact group of faint stars, Coma Berenices, the Hair of Berenice.

VIRGO AND HER GALAXIES

To the ancient myth-spinners, Virgo was not the Christian Virgin Mary but a corn goddess, usually depicted with wings and carrying an ear of corn. She can also be the goddess of justice, with her scales represented by Libra nearby. Virgo covers a large area of sky, and is the second-largest constellation after Hydra (the Water Snake) which winds to her south, starting near Cancer and ending near Libra.

This part of the sky is fairly empty of stars, because it is well away from the line of the Milky Way. At this time of year we are looking out of the plane of the Galaxy, but instead of stars there are galaxies. The bowl of the "Y" of Virgo is known as the "Realm of the Galaxies" and detailed star maps show them crowded together in this area. This is known as the Virgo Cluster, and to appreciate it you have to step outside our own galaxy and see the wider picture. The Milky Way Galaxy is in an outlying group, known as the Local Group (see pages 22), on the fringes of the Virgo Cluster. This contains thousands of galaxies, with several giant elliptical galaxies at its center, notably M87.

ASTRO FACT

The galaxy M87 has a supermassive black hole at its center, with a mass 3 billion times that of the Sun.

Virgo Cluster

Sadly, because of the distance of the Virgo Cluster (about 50 million light-years), a casual glance at the Realm of the Galaxies with binoculars is a disappointment. With care you can spot a few of them from good country locations, but they are tiny, faint, and fuzzy.

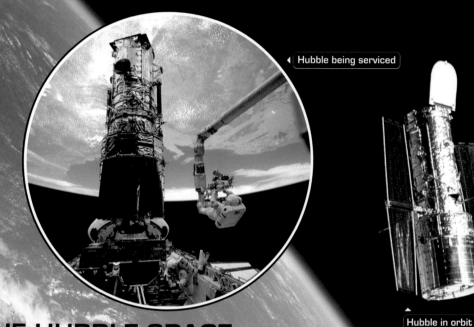

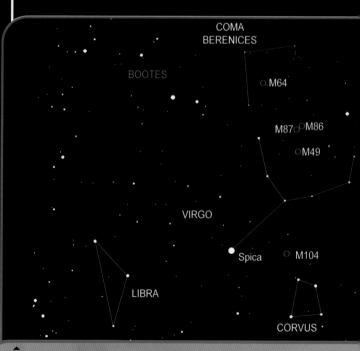

Hubble being serviced

Hubble in orbit

THE COMA STAR CLUSTER

The Virgo Cluster extends into Coma Berenices, to Virgo's north. The reason why the constellation has long been associated with locks of hair is the glittering star cluster within it, which by its shape does indeed resemble a flowing head of hair. It's easily visible with the naked eye as a close group of about 20 stars, and it fills the field of view of binoculars with glowing points of light. The cluster lies about 290 light-years away.

THE HUBBLE SPACE TELESCOPE

One of the main purposes of the Hubble Space Telescope was to measure accurately the distance to the Virgo Cluster. Only a telescope in space could pick out a few individual stars in galaxies so far away, so that their properties could be measured and compared with similar stars in our own galaxy. Though Hubble is not a particularly large telescope, with a 2.4 meter diameter mirror, it has the great advantage that in space its view is not affected by our own turbulent atmosphere, and it can spend many hours or even days photographing particularly faint objects. Hubble has proved itself to be an invaluable tool, and by spotting stars in Virgo Cluster galaxies it has enabled astronomers to fix the distance scale of the whole universe much more precisely. It has been upgraded several times over the years by astronauts from the Space Shuttle, and is due to be replaced in about 2013.

COMA
BERENICES

BOOTES

○ M64

M87 ○ ○ M86

○ M49

VIRGO

Spica   ○ M104

LIBRA

CORVUS

Sky highlights
All the objects circled are galaxies in the Virgo Cluster at about 50 million light-years distance, except for M64, in Coma Berenices, which is about 12 million light-years away from the Milky Way.

45

CRUX AND CENTAURUS

The Southern Cross is a symbol of the southern hemisphere, and can only be seen properly south of the Tropics. It turns around the south celestial pole, so from April to July evenings it is high in the sky, while from September to January it is low down. It is recognizable from the two bright stars, Alpha and Beta Centauri, that point to it on its east side.

The Southern Cross and the Coalsack, shown in a long-exposure photograph

CRUX

The Southern Cross is not an ancient constellation, though in ancient times it was visible from the Mediterranean area as a result of precession—the slow wobble of the Earth's axis. Then it was regarded as part of Centaurus. It was the early European voyagers who saw the clear and compact crucifix pattern and named it separately. Its Latin name, Crux, simply means "The Cross" though it is invariably referred to as "The Southern Cross."

It is the smallest constellation, and northerners may be surprised by how compact it is. Its stars are bright, but southern-hemisphere skies are rich in bright stars and it can sometimes get lost among them all. There is another larger and fainter cross shape made up of four stars in nearby Carina and Vela, so to make sure you have the true Cross look for the very bright stars Alpha and Beta Centauri to its east, known as the Pointers, as they do point to it.

There is a star cluster, famously dubbed the Jewel Box, near the Cross star that is closest to the Pointers. But this is more spectacular in a telescope than in binoculars as it is very compact. More obvious in good skies is the large dark nebula known as the Coalsack, just to the south of this. It really does look like a hole in the Milky Way.

ASTRO FACT

Alpha Centauri is the nearest bright star to the Sun. It lies just over four light-years away: not particularly close by Milky Way standards. A telescope shows two stars, one slightly brighter than the Sun and one slightly fainter. They orbit each other every 80 years. But the actual nearest star is a very faint outlying member of the system, Proxima. This is slightly closer, at 4.22 light-years.

CENTAURUS

This constellation occupies a large area of sky south of Virgo and Libra and much of it is visible from the southern United States. It does not have an easily recognized shape, but its two brightest stars are the Pointers, Alpha and Beta Centauri, often known by those names though they can also be called Rigil Kent and Hadar. The centaur is a mythological beast, half man, half horse, and the celestial one is meant to be Chiron, tutor to the gods. One of the stars of Centarurus, Omega, is obviously fuzzy to the naked eye. In reality it is a globular cluster, a type of star cluster quite different from the more familiar ones such as the Pleiades. Globular clusters are found around the fringes of the Milky Way Galaxy, and are quite distant. They can contain hundreds of thousand stars rather then just a hundred or so, in a spherical shape. Most globulars are too faint to be seen with the naked eye, but Omega Centauri is the exception. Binoculars show it as a hazy blob, but a telescope is needed to show individual stars.

Omega Centauri

◀ Centaurus, as depicted in a Japanese rendering

• CENTAURUS

○NGC 5128

○Omega Centauri

LUPUS

CRUX

NGC 4755○

Alpha Centauri   Beta Centauri

The galaxy NGC 5128 is an elliptical galaxy with a dark band which is part of another galaxy in collision with it.

▲
Sky highlights
Omega Centauri is the brightest globular cluster, 16,000 light-years away. NGC 4755 is the Jewel Box Cluster, so named because of a red star within it. NGC 5128 is a colliding galaxy, just visible with binoculars as a tiny smudge of light.

47

CYGNUS AND LYRA

The North America Nebula (left) and the fainter Pelican Nebula to its right

A triangle of bright stars occupies the skies from July to October. Known in the northern hemisphere as the Summer Triangle, it consists of Vega, Altair, and Deneb. The latter marks one end of the cross-shape of Cygnus, also referred to as the Northern Cross. Though the opposite end has only a fairly faint star, it is an easy shape to find and, together with the other stars of the Triangle, is a useful signpost to the other constellations in the area, some of which are quite small, such as Vulpecula and Sagitta.

Summer Triangle ▶

CYGNUS, THE SWAN

This swan, flying down the Milky Way, is the shape-shifting god Zeus in one of his many disguises, in amorous pursuit as usual. Deneb marks the swan's tail, its outstretched wings are the arms of the cross, and its long neck points southward, with the star Albireo at its head. It is in a rich and interesting part of the Milky Way, packed with stars. Deneb is a real searchlight of a star, and is the most distant bright star in the sky, at over 1,400 light-years. It is about 60,000 times as bright as the Sun. Close to Deneb is the North America Nebula, so called because of its shape. This is so large and spectacular in photographs that you might imagine it would be an easy sight in binoculars. Actually it is visible with the naked eye, but only as a brighter patch of the Milky Way—the red color does not show up to the eye. With binoculars, in a dark sky you can trace out the dark lane starting near Deneb that marks out the East Coast, leading on to the Gulf of Mexico. The nebula is just the visible edge of a massive dark nebula visible to the naked eye as the Great Rift, which stretches all the way down to Sagittarius.

THE DISTANCES OF THE STARS

The star 61 Cygni, which makes a quadrilateral with Deneb and the eastern arm of the Cross, drew attention to itself in the nineteenth century, moving particularly rapidly through the sky—equivalent to a fifth of the Moon's diameter in a century. In 1838 the German astronomer Friedrich Bessel measured its parallax, which is the slight apparent movement caused by the Earth's own movement as it orbits the Sun. This put its distance at around 11 light-years. Parallax remains the only accurate means of measuring a star's distance.

Part of the Veil Nebula supernova remnant

VEIL NEBULA

Another famous object lies in Cygnus—the Veil Nebula. This is the remnant of a supernova that exploded maybe 50,000 years ago, and which is now visible as a shell of material about 2 degrees across (four times the diameter of the full Moon). Photographs bring out delicate wreaths of gas, although it's best seen through a good telescope equipped with a suitable filter that cuts out all but the light from the nebula.

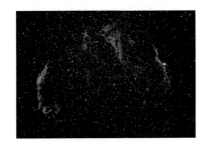

LYRA, THE LYRE

The only musical instrument provided for the gods in the sky is the lyre. Its bright star, Vega, is the fifth brightest in the night sky. Though it is three times brighter in the sky than Deneb, this is because it is comparatively close, at 25 light-years, and some 37 times brighter than the Sun. Near Vega is the double star Epsilon Lyrae. Good eyesight will reveal that it is two stars, but with a telescope you can see that each of the pair is itself a double, leading to its popular name of the "Double Double." Between Beta and Gamma Lyrae is another of those must-see objects in the sky, particularly if you have a telescope. This is the Ring Nebula, a planetary nebula in the shape of a slightly flattened doughnut. It's notoriously hard to judge the distances of planetary nebulae, but this one is judged to be about 2,300 light-years away.

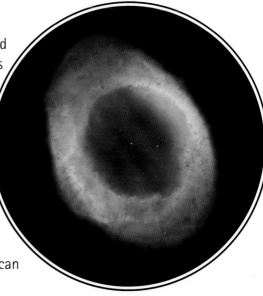

The Ring Nebula, photographed by the Hubble Space Telescope.

Sky highlights
M57 is the Ring Nebula, which is visible using small telescopes. NGC 6992 is the brightest part of the Veil Nebula. NGC 7000 is the North America Nebula.

SCORPIUS

From the northern hemisphere, the distinctive pattern of Scorpius is low in the south at this time of year, while from many southern-hemisphere locations it is virtually overhead. Look for Antares, an orange star with stars on either side of it, which is at one end of a long curve of stars, in the line of the Milky Way. Don't confuse it with Altair, farther north, which also has similar stars on either side but is white and has no other bright stars nearby.

Globular cluster M4

ASTRO FACT

Other clusters in Scorpius include the globular cluster M4 (above), looking like a fuzzy ball in binoculars, and NGC 6231, near the southern bend in the scorpion's tail.

Today, only a short part of the Sun's path passes through Scorpius, so the Sun actually spends only five days within the constellation. Instead, it passes through Ophiuchus.

SCORPION IN THE SKY

Constellation figure ▶ of Scorpius

Legend has it that the great Orion was killed by a scorpion, and here it is. But to avoid further accidents, Scorpius is placed as far away from Orion as possible. In fact, as it rises in the east Orion slips quietly down into the west, and it sets just as Orion starts to appear again.

This is one of those constellations that really does resemble what it's meant to be, and as often happens it is one of the oldest. With Antares at its heart and a long, upraised sting, Scorpius is unmistakable, though from more northerly locations some of its tail is very low in the sky or never even rises. This is one of the richest parts of the sky for star clusters, some of which are visible with the naked eye.

The most prominent pair are M6 and M7, which lie between the sting and Sagittarius. To the naked eye they are misty patches that invite you to turn the binoculars on them. These will show individual stars in the clusters, and you will probably be able to see both in the same field of view—a breathtaking sight in a good sky. M6, which is the closer to Antares in the sky, is sometimes called the Butterfly Cluster because of the pattern of its stars as seen in binoculars.

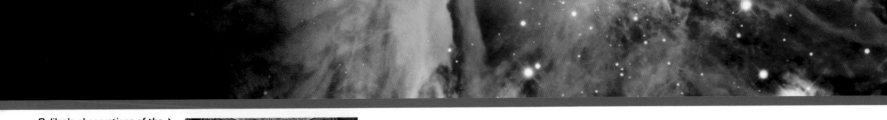

Galileo's observations of the ▶ Milky Way revealed its true nature for the first time

GALILEO AND THE TELESCOPE

The Milky Way in Scorpius and surrounding areas is packed with stars. Binoculars or a telescope show these well, and it's a great treat on a good, clear night to scan along the line of the Milky Way. The larger the telescope, the more you see. But it was not until the invention of the telescope about 400 years ago that this was first realized. Until then, the Milky Way was just a mysterious hazy band stretching across the sky. Mythology claimed that it was milk spilt when the goddess Hera was suckling Heracles, a mortal son of Zeus. That it was composed of countless stars was one of the first discoveries announced by the Italian scientist Galileo in 1610.

Galileo had used an early telescope to observe the heavens, and also found that the Moon has mountains and a cratered surface, that Venus shows phases, and that Jupiter has satellites moving around it. These announcements caused a great stir, as they contradicted the long-held belief that the Earth was the center of the Universe, yet here was Galileo saying that Venus went around the Sun and that Jupiter was the center of its own retinue of moons.
Eventually, of course, Galileo was vindicated.

◀ The Milky Way from Cygnus at top down to Scorpius

Closeup of M6
▼

Closeup of M7
▼

SCORPIUS

Antares M4

M6
M7

NGC 6231

Sky highlights
M6 is 1,600 light-years away and M7 is half that distance. NGC 6231 is 5,600 light-years away and M4 is 7,200 light-years away.

SAGITTARIUS

The most recognizable part of Sagittarius is a group of seven or so stars in the obvious shape of a teapot (as seen from the northern hemisphere). If you can find Antares in Scorpius (see page 50), the Teapot lies to its east. From northern-hemisphere locations, Sagittarius is close to the southern horizon, but from the southern hemisphere, during evenings in June to September, it is more or less overhead.

◀ The Milky Way is brightest in Sagittarius, although the actual center of the Galaxy is hidden by dust clouds that show up dark in this long-exposure photo.

Lagoon Nebula, M8 ▶

SECOND CENTAUR

Sagittarius, the archer, is represented as a centaur, even though the sky already has a perfectly good one (see page 47). Two legends seem to have become confused and some say that this should represent an archer on horseback. The archer in question may have been Crotus, the inventor of archery. Curiously for such a starry part of the sky, none of the stars in Sagittarius is particularly bright. This is the most southerly of the constellations of the Zodiac, and from the more northerly locations is only visible for a few hours in the night close to the horizon, which spoils much of the splendor of the Milky Way in this area. Scanning with binoculars reveals a number of hazy areas, either nebulae or clusters, and Sagittarius has the greatest number of such objects of all the constellations. There are star clusters such as M23 and M25, nebulae such as the Lagoon Nebula, and globular clusters such as M22. If it were not in Sagittarius, with its wealth of other objects, this cluster would be better known.

NEBULAE IN SAGITTARIUS

One of the most obvious misty patches in Sagittarius is a nebula, the Lagoon Nebula, also known as M8. It gets its name from a dark lane visible within it, which reminded an imaginative nineteenth-century astronomer of a lagoon, though photographs don't really show this appearance. To its north lies the Trifid Nebula, M20, so called because of three dark lanes within it dividing it into three—the name means "cleft in three." To photographers this is a colorful target, with one part being pink hydrogen gas, and the other being a blue nebula, the result of light from a blue star reflecting off a dust cloud. However, despite its dramatic appearance in photographs, the Trifid Nebula is not easy to see as the eye is not very sensitive to its red color.

THE BLACK HEART OF THE GALAXY

The center of the Galaxy lies in Sagittarius, so you might think this would be a brilliant spot. But although there is a bright part of the Milky Way in Sagittarius, known as the Sagittarius Star Cloud, the direction of the actual center is hidden by dust clouds. It takes radiotelescopes and satellites to reveal what lies there. A strong source of radio waves is being orbited by several stars, but no light comes from the spot they are orbiting. Analyzing their motion yields the amazing result that the object has a mass around three to four million times that of the Sun, yet it is less than the diameter of the Solar System! It is almost certainly a supermassive black hole. Many other galaxies are also found to have such objects at their centers.

Infrared photo of stars at the center of the Galaxy
▼

Trifid Nebula, M20
▲

○M25   ○M23

○M22   ○M20
         ○M8

SAGITTARIUS

▲ Sky highlights
M8 is the Lagoon Nebula while M20 is the Trifid. M22 is a bright globular cluster, and M23 and M25 are star clusters easily visible with binoculars.

53

THE AQUILA REGION

Within the triangle of Deneb, Vega, and Altair lie several small constellations that contain no bright stars but have a number of interesting objects. Immediately north of Altair is an arrow-shaped group, Sagitta. Between there and the star marking the head of Cygnus lies Vulpecula, while to the east of Altair is a pretty pattern representing Delphinus. And to the southwest of Altair is a C-shape of stars on the edge of Scutum.

Closeup of the Coathanger
▼

REALM OF THE EAGLE

Altair is the main star of Aquila, the Eagle, the bird that in mythology carried the thunderbolts for Zeus. The constellation itself is unremarkable, despite being in the Milky Way. North of it, Sagitta represents an arrow that seems to have missed both the eagle and Cygnus, the Swan. Despite its small size and faintness, Sagitta is an ancient constellation and it features in several Greek legends.

You can use Sagitta to locate one of the largest and best-known planetary nebulae in the sky with binoculars. Put the brightest star of Sagitta at the southern edge of the field of view, and near the northern edge lies the Dumbbell Nebula, M27. It gets its name from its twin-lobed shape as seen in a small telescope. Planetary nebulae are so called because they often show pale disks, just like distant planets seen through a telescope, rather than because they have anything to do with the formation of planets. The object is in the constellation of Vulpecula, the Fox.

Going back to Sagitta, now put the tail of the arrow at the southeastern edge of the field of view and at the opposite edge lies a group of stars that has a great popularity among stargazers—the group known as the Coathanger, in Vulpecula. This little line of stars with a hook shape in the middle is mostly a chance alignment, but its shape often delights observers.

The Dumbbell Nebula as photographed by an amateur astronomer

ASTRO FACT
Vulpecula was originally known as *Vulpecula et Anser*—the Fox and Goose. But the goose seems to have gone—maybe eaten by the fox!

◀ Nineteenth-century star atlas illustration showing Delphinus, Aquila, and Sagitta

ABOUT TELESCOPES

Many people wish they had a telescope that allows them to look at the wonders of the sky. In general, the larger the aperture (the diameter of the main lens or mirror) the brighter and more detailed the view. For occasional stargazing, a refracting telescope is fine, ideally one of three inches aperture or more.

Four-inch ▶ reflecting telescope

Reflecting telescopes are better value in the larger sizes, particularly six inches and greater, but the mirrors require more care and maintenance. Some telescopes, called catadioptrics, are a cross between the two types, containing both lenses and mirrors for compactness. Many are computer-controlled and will find objects automatically, but stargazers often prefer to find objects themselves.

ANCIENT CONSTELLATION

Delphinus, the Dolphin, really does look like a dolphin leaping out of the water. It is an ancient constellation, unlike Scutum, the Shield, which was introduced in 1684 by the Polish astronomer Hevelius. Just at the southern tip of the C-shape of stars in Aquila is a compact star cluster, the Wild Duck Cluster, cataloged as M11. In a small telescope, you might be able to pick out the V-shape of stars that gives it its popular name.

◀ This small refracting telescope is on an equatorial mount that allows you to track the stars easily.

Sky highlights
Cr 399 stands for Collinder 399—better known as the Coathanger.
M11 is the Wild Duck Cluster and M27 is the Dumbbell Nebula.

55

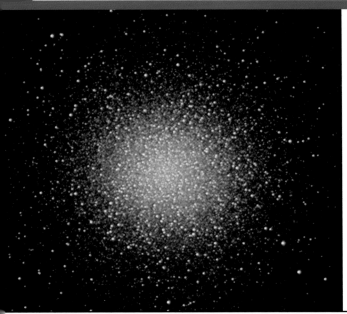

These constellations don't fit into such neat patterns as some others because their stars are widely spaced. One easily located pattern is the "Keystone" of Hercules, which is midway between the star Vega and the semicircle of stars of Corona Borealis. Another is a line of four stars to the north of Antares, including a close pair, which form one branch of the pattern of Ophiuchus. Continue this line and you come to a triangle of stars in the head of Serpens, the Serpent.

◄ M13, the "Great Cluster" in Hercules

HERCULES THE HERO

Hercules is the Latin name of the Greek hero Heracles, who was required to carry out 12 labors, some of which are celebrated in other sky myths. But in the sky he is not particularly impressive, and is even ignominiously shown upside down, though this allows him to rest his foot on the head of Draco, the dragon, which he slew.

The "Keystone" shape is easily spotted if you look in the right spot, and this allows you to find what's sometimes called the Great Cluster—the globular cluster M13, which lies along its western edge. It is only "great" compared to some of the other globular clusters in the northern hemisphere, and is not a patch on the bright globulars south of the equator. It's just visible with the naked eye, and in binoculars you can see a fuzzy ball, which in fact is something like a third of a million stars packed into a space about 100 light-years across. By comparison, in the same volume of the Sun's neighborhood there are only about 1,700 stars, most of them very faint!

TAURUS PONIATOWSKI, SERPENTARIUS. Pl.12

▲ Ophiuchus and Serpens, from a nineteenth-century sky atlas

THE PILLARS OF CREATION

In binoculars, the Eagle Nebula is disappointing. Telescopes show a few dark patches near its center that faintly resemble an eagle with partially open wings. But it was not until the area was photographed by the Hubble Space Telescope in 1995 that it became famous. The photograph revealed the dark nebula to consist of long trunks of dense gas, surrounded by brighter gas. Astronomers interpreted the columns as being the birthplace of stars, and dubbed them the "Pillars of Creation." Stars that have already formed are helping to burn away the gas from the outside of the columns, giving them their almost solid appearance.

The "Pillars of Creation" from the Hubble Space Telescope shows a closeup of the eagle shape.
▼

OPHIUCHUS AND THE SERPENT

The constellation of Ophiuchus, the Serpent-bearer, represents Aesclepius, the god of medicine. To this day, the sign of a serpent coiled round a stick is used by the medical profession. The serpent itself, Serpens, actually appears in the sky with its head, known as Serpens Caput, to the northwest of Ophiuchus, while its tail, Serpens Cauda, is next to Scutum.

▲
An Earth-based photo of the Eagle Nebula, with the shape of the eagle at its center.

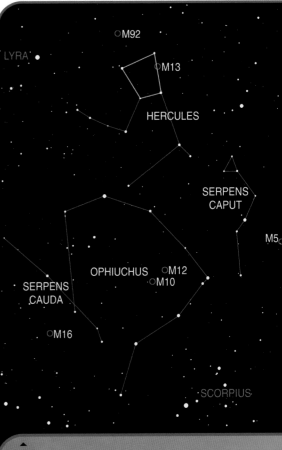

▲
Sky highlights
M16 is the Eagle Nebula, though despite its fame it is not an easy object visually. All the other marked objects are globular clusters, of which M13 is the brightest, visible using binoculars.

SOUTH POLAR SKY

The stars on this map are always due south—all that changes is their orientation. The center of the map is always the same angle above your horizon as your latitude, which means that from most of the northern hemisphere, this part of the sky is always below the horizon. From most cities in Australia, New Zealand, and South Africa, the Southern Cross is usually visible.

Eta Carinae Nebula, with the ▶
complete nebula inset.

CARINA

Carina is the keel of the ship Argo. It is a gem of a constellation, though it does not have a neat pattern like many others. Its leading star, Canopus, is the second brightest in the night sky but lies some way from the rest of the constellation's brighter stars, which are close to the Southern Cross.

The brightest nebula in the sky, the Eta Carinae Nebula, is easy to spot by using the shorter arm of the Southern Cross as a signpost. It is easily visible with the naked eye, and binoculars will show you the dark lane within it that is very obvious in photographs of the object. It surrounds the star Eta Carinae which is now on the limit of visibility with the naked eye, but which has been known to flare up brilliantly. It is one of the most massive stars known, and may well provide a surprise in the future.

Crux

FINDING SOUTH

Unlike the north polar sky, there is no bright star that happens to be close to the celestial pole, marking the direction of south. But you can use the Southern Cross, when it is visible, to give you a rough guide. The long axis of the Cross points almost due south, and four-and-a-half Cross lengths

THE MAGELLANIC CLOUDS

The south polar sky has two features not seen anywhere else in the sky: the Large and Small Magellanic Clouds (often referred to as the LMC and SMC). These look very like fragments torn off the Milky Way, both in brightness and appearance, but they are actually separate galaxies beyond our own. They are small irregular galaxies close to the Milky Way Galaxy, and are part of our Local Group which also contains the Andromeda Galaxy. They are much closer to us than Andromeda, at about 170,000 light-years for the LMC and 190,000 for the SMC. You can't see individual stars in either, even with binoculars, though the LMC in particular does have mottling as a result of nebulae and clusters within it. Close to the SMC is what appears to be a fuzzy star. This is the bright globular cluster 47 Tucanae, a woolly ball in binoculars but resolved into stars with a telescope, much closer than the SMC at 13,400 light-years.

Closeup of the Southern Pleiades in Carina. The brightest star is Theta Carinae.

SOUTHERN PLEIADES

Your eyes may be attracted to a little group of stars surrounding the star Theta Carinae. This cluster, cataloged as IC 2602, is also known as the "Southern Pleiades" because of a similarity to that famous cluster. There are several other delightful clusters in Carina, notably NGC 3532, just to the east of Eta Carinae, and NGC 2516.

VIEWING THE MAP

With the current month at the bottom, the map shows the sky looking south at midnight. Turn it one month clockwise for every two hours earlier. The horizon will cut across some of the lower part of the map. The farther north you are, the higher it will be on the map (see diagram, page 21).

◀ Sky highlights
LMC is the Large Magellanic Cloud and SMC is the Small Magellanic Cloud. IC 2602 is the Southern Pleiades. NGC 2516 is a bright star cluster easily visible with the naked eye, while 47 Tucanae is a bright globular cluster.

REFERENCES & CREDITS

FINDING OUT MORE

If you want a more detailed star chart, and to find out more about amateur astronomy and telescopes, you need the Astro-Pack by Robin Scagell, published by Thunder Bay Press (ISBN 978-1-59223-089-X). It also contains a planisphere or star-wheel, which you can set for any date and time to show the whole sky.

USEFUL WEB SITES

For further information about topics covered in this book please go to the author's website, **www.stargazing.org.uk**, which also gives advice on choosing a telescope.

NASA SITES

You can keep up-to-date with the latest planetary and manned missions by going to **www.nasa.gov** and follow the links provided there.

Information about manned United States space missions can be found at spaceflight.nasa gov. Images from current space flights are posted there.

Photos from planetary missions are posted at **photojournal.jpl.nasa.gov**. The opening menu gives you a choice of planet, and in each case the most recent images are displayed first. Photos from many previous missions can be found there.

To find a selection of the best images from NASA, go to the Great Images in NASA site at **grin.hq.nasa.gov**.

The Hubble Space Telescope's web site is **www.stsci.edu/outreach**. There you can find out more about Hubble and its successor, the James Webb Space Telescope, and download all the publicly released images.

RESOURCES ON THE WEB

Earth satellites can often be spotted, but how do you know where and when to look? The site at **www.heavens-above.com** allows you to discover what bright satellites are visible from any location you choose. Look in particular for the section on Iridium flares. These are bright flashes from moving satellites in the Iridium satellite communications network, which can be predicted very accurately.

Another useful prediction site is **www.calsky.com**. Here you can find information about the planets and their current positions.

For a free and attractive sky viewer that you can download, go to **www.stellarium.org**. This will show you a realistic view of the sky from anywhere in the world.

The Society for Popular Astronomy in the UK has a lively and informative web site. Go to **www.popastro.com**.

Sky and Telescope is a leading monthly astronomy magazine with a site, **www.skyandtelescope.com**, that carries lots of up-to-date news about what's in the sky.

Another useful site is **www.spaceweather.com**. Here you can find out about transient events such as aurorae, sunspots and asteroids that pass close to the Earth.

CREDITS